ARTIFICIAL INTELLIGENCE IN THE REAL WORLD

by George Anthony Kulz

FOCUS READERS.

VOYAGER

www.focusreaders.com

Focus Readers is distributed by North Star Editions:
sales@northstareditions.com | 888-417-0195

Produced for Focus Readers by Red Line Editorial.

Content Consultant: Magy Seif El-Nasr, Associate Professor of Khoury College of Computer Sciences, Northeastern University

Photographs ©: Alexandre Ovcharov/Sputnik/AP Images, cover, 1; Anton Gvozdikov/Shutterstock Images, 4–5; paparazzza/Shutterstock Images, 7; Kin Cheung/AP Images, 9; Ronny Hartmann/picture-alliance/dpa/AP Images, 10–11; Mark Genito/AP Images, 13; Maridav/Shutterstock Images, 15; Yellow Cat/Shutterstock Images, 16–17; Red Line Editorial, 19, 27; Ned Snowman/Shutterstock Images, 21; wellphoto/Shutterstock Images, 22–23; Surasak_Photo/Shutterstock Images, 25; Bao feng/ICHPL Imaginechina/AP Images, 28–29; Michael Fitzsimmons/Shutterstock Images, 31; Kenny Crookston/AP Images, 33; Hiroshi Arimitsu/Yomiuru Shimbun/AP Images, 34–35; Quality Stock Arts/Shutterstock Images, 37; aslysun/Shutterstock Images, 38; FrameStockFootages/Shutterstock Images, 40–41; ICHPL Imaginechina/AP Images, 43; Timothy A. Clary/AFP/Getty Images, 45

Library of Congress Cataloging-in-Publication Data
Names: Kulz, George Anthony, author.
Title: Artificial intelligence in the real world / by George Anthony Kulz.
Description: Lake Elmo, MN : Focus Readers, 2020. | Series: Artificial
    intelligence | Includes index. | Audience: Grades 7–9
Identifiers: LCCN 2019032156 (print) | LCCN 2019032157 (ebook) | ISBN
    9781644930748 (hardcover) | ISBN 9781644931530 (paperback) | ISBN
    9781644933114 (ebook pdf) | ISBN 9781644932322 (hosted ebook)
Subjects: LCSH: Artificial intelligence--Juvenile literature. | Artificial
    intelligence--Medical applications--Juvenile literature. | Artificial
    intelligence--Industrial applications--Juvenile literature.
Classification: LCC Q335.4 .K85 2020 (print) | LCC Q335.4 (ebook) | DDC
    006.3--dc23
LC record available at https://lccn.loc.gov/2019032156
LC ebook record available at https://lccn.loc.gov/2019032157

Printed in the United States of America
Mankato, MN
012020

ABOUT THE AUTHOR

George Anthony Kulz holds a master's degree in computer engineering. He is a member of the Society of Children's Book Writers and Illustrators and has taken courses at the Institute of Children's Literature and the Gotham Writers' Workshop. He writes for children and adults.

TABLE OF CONTENTS

CHAPTER 1

INTRODUCTION TO AI

On October 25, 2017, a robot named Sophia became the first non-human citizen of a country. Saudi Arabia accepted her as one of its own. Sophia was now the most famous robot in the world. She was invited to speak at conventions and on talk shows. She answered questions about how robots and people can help one another. And she stood up for women's rights.

Sophia speaks before a crowd at the Open Innovations Conference in October 2017.

Sophia looked, spoke, and acted like a real woman. But she was one of the most advanced robots in the world. The United Nations, a group of countries working together for world peace, even gave her an assignment. The organization asked her to find ways to improve the world by using technology.

Sophia is an example of artificial intelligence (AI). AI refers to the building of intelligent machines that can reason, learn, and even mimic some human behaviors. For example, some robots with AI use sensors to avoid objects and recognize faces. Other robots with AI can walk, climb stairs, and jump. A few, like Sophia, may even appear to have emotions. But experts debate whether robots can ever have real emotions.

AI is not just about smart robots. Many of the devices people use every day involve AI.

▲ Students interact with the human-like robot Sophia.

Some AI programs analyze data. They learn to associate one thing with another. They plan and predict events. Other AI programs use data to solve problems. AI helps police departments fight crime. It helps people make purchases and manage money. And it helps build products in factories. AI is all around us.

DAVID HANSON

Sophia is an invention of Hanson Robotics. Dr. David Hanson founded this company in 2003. Dr. Hanson didn't start out as an AI researcher. He received a bachelor's degree in film, animation, and video. He later earned a doctorate in **interactive** arts and engineering from the University of Texas at Dallas. His first job was at Disney. He built sculptures and robots for Disney's theme parks.

Sophia is special because she is the first AI citizen. However, Hanson Robotics built other robots before Sophia. Each robot advanced the field of AI. For example, the face of the Albert HUBO robot resembles physicist Albert Einstein. It was the first **android** AI robot that could make human facial expressions. BINA48 is an AI robot that acts like a real person named Bina Rothblatt. It has Rothblatt's memories and personality.

David Hanson works on the robot Sophia one month before she was granted Saudi Arabian citizenship.

It can speak with anyone who talks to it. And it can change facial expressions.

Some people worry that human-like robots will trigger the uncanny valley effect. In this effect, people react negatively to robots that appear human but fail to perfectly mimic human movement and behavior. The robots seem both familiar and strange, making people feel uneasy. Dr. Hanson does not share this concern. He started Hanson Robotics with the goal of building realistic robots to exist alongside humans.

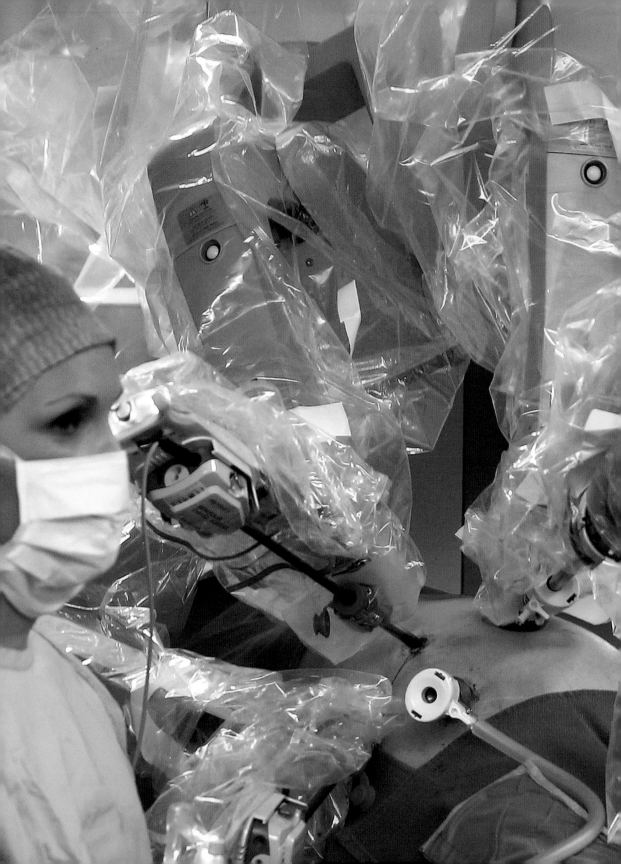

CHAPTER 2

AI AND HEALTH CARE

Artificial intelligence has been involved in health care for decades. Doctors have been using AI to diagnose patients since the 1980s. Expert systems are a form of AI that make decisions about patient care. **Programmers** give these systems a knowledge base of medical facts. The systems interpret and evaluate those facts to provide a diagnosis. But AI is useful for more than diagnostics.

A surgeon directs the da Vinci surgical system to perform surgery in 2019.

Today, developers are making strides in AI and robotics usage in health care. Robots with AI are becoming more common in hospitals and doctors' offices. Some of them help with surgeries. For example, in 2019, scientists used a tiny robot to find and repair a leaky valve in a patient's heart. Larger robots perform tasks such as carrying supplies and blood samples. A hospital in San Francisco, California, has robots called Tugs that know the hospital's hallways. They sense when people and other **obstacles** are in their way.

Some AI programs make important decisions for medical staff. AI programs help assign beds at Johns Hopkins Hospital in Baltimore, Maryland. They look at available beds and a list of patients' symptoms. Then they figure out which patients can be assigned to which beds. AI programs are also used to handle documentation. They know

▲ A Tug robot pulls medical supplies through a hospital in 2004.

rules for recording patient data and can enter data into patients' records. Their help frees up doctors and nurses to work with patients instead of spending time on documentation.

Scientists are using AI to develop new medications. Computers with AI study people's cells. With that knowledge, they create medicine to treat diseases. One example is an AI program called AtomNet. It can find new medicines 100 times faster than a **pharmaceutical** company can. Because of its quick work, these medicines can be brought to market faster. Patients can be treated with these new medicines sooner.

AI also helps people take care of their own health. Wearable devices and apps check heart rate, blood pressure, and sleep patterns. Based on this information, the apps recommend ways

➤ THINK ABOUT IT

AI can do common jobs such as carrying supplies and resource planning in medical facilities. Why might some workers worry about this?

People can wear smart watches to track their own fitness.

the users can stay healthy. Other apps figure out if a problem is important enough to see a doctor. Based on a list of symptoms, these apps guess what might be wrong with someone.

Although AI does a lot for health care, it is not perfect. AI can only base its decisions on what it has learned. Also, robots with AI do not have emotions like people do. They cannot provide the emotional care patients may need. Human doctors and nurses are still important in health care.

CHAPTER 3

DOING BUSINESS WITH AI

Many businesses have started using AI. Some AI programs work directly with customers in stores and hotels. They help people buy products they're interested in. Other AI programs work behind the scenes in stores and warehouses. They assist business owners and workers with their jobs. And anyone who has bought something online has likely come in contact with an AI system.

Toshiba's Junko Chihira robot works in a visitor information center in Japan.

More and more businesses are using AI to advertise to customers. AI software keeps track of the social media sites people visit. It gathers data about customers' likes and dislikes, their spending habits, and what products they've bought. Businesses can use that data. They can send people ads about products they might be interested in.

AI performs a similar job in the banking and financial world. Many banks and financial institutions use AI **chatbots** to help customers with simple banking needs. These programs talk to customers in a variety of ways, including over

➤ THINK ABOUT IT

To do business with humans, AI programs collect a lot of information about people. What are the advantages and disadvantages of this data collection?

the phone and on banking websites. The chatbots act like people, which customers like. But they also work faster and cheaper than people do, which businesses like. They even learn customers' activities and suggest services to them.

Offline, robots and other AI programs are starting to appear in more customer service jobs. They are replacing cashiers in some stores.

PERSONAL DATA MINING ◄

Through a process called data mining, AI software analyzes the data it collects about people. It finds patterns in the data. Businesses use these patterns to send people targeted ads.

Online Habits		Targeted Ads
Hannah buys shoes from an online store.	→	Ads from shoe companies appear in Hannah's Facebook feed.
Alisha regularly buys books on Amazon.	→	Alisha receives emails from Amazon suggesting other books she might be interested in.
Joel watches cartoons on a streaming site.	→	Ads for the cartoon and similar shows appear on other websites that Joel visits.

Stores such as Amazon Go in Seattle, Washington, have no checkout counters at all. Customers simply scan an app when they enter the store. An AI system keeps track of everything they buy. When customers leave the store, they are automatically charged for what they bought.

Another business where AI systems wait on customers is the Henn na Hotel in Japan. Robots assist with checking in and bringing luggage to rooms. In this hotel, guests do not need keys. AI software recognizes guests' faces before allowing them into their rooms. In early 2019, some of the robots had to be "fired." Some were unable to answer customers' questions. Others could only carry luggage when the weather was good. AI is still a new technology and is not perfect. However, the hotel is an example of where AI might be headed in the future.

▲ A dinosaur-robot receptionist checks people in at the Henn na Hotel in Japan.

AI does more than help customers. It also helps businesses run more efficiently. Some warehouses are becoming fully **automated**. For example, an online retailer in China has an entire warehouse of AI-powered robots. These robots can take packages from conveyor belts and box them for shipping. No people are needed except to repair the robots if there is a problem.

CHAPTER 4

AI IN MANUFACTURING

Robots have been used in **manufacturing** plants since the 1950s. Those early robots worked in controlled environments. They needed pages of instructions before they could build a product. And they did the same tasks over and over.

In contrast, new robots with AI analyze 3D models of what a product looks like. Then they figure out how to build the product on their own.

Many businesses use robots with AI in factories.

Robots with AI check products for problems. They decide how products are delivered. They also figure out how resources are used in factories.

In most factories, a group of people ensures products are made correctly. This group is called quality assurance, or QA. However, AI is beginning to take on that role. AI programs can be trained to know what a product is supposed to look like. When the programs see a product that looks different, they can identify that product as being bad. AI programs can also act as QA for other AI and machines in the factory. They can estimate when machines will need maintenance or replacing. Some AI programs have sensors that can check if any machine parts are failing.

Factories also use AI to improve the supply chain. A supply chain is the process of building products and then sending them to stores and

A robot creates a printed circuit board for use in an electronic device.

warehouses. AI programs can examine large amounts of data. They look at pricing, weather data, and how many customers visit a particular store. Then the programs change how and when products are delivered. AI programs also help with resource planning. They figure out how many workers and materials are needed to build products.

Some AI factories are run almost entirely by robots. They are known as lights-out factories. They can be run without lights or other expensive features needed by human workers. Lights-out factories allow companies to save money. One lights-out factory has robots that make other robots. There are no people in the entire factory.

Not all factories are using AI to replace humans. Some factories use AI to help workers. In car plants, for example, automated guided vehicles (AGVs) carry materials from place to place. AGVs let people focus on building cars. They also prevent people from having to do heavy lifting.

Exoskeletons with AI can also help people work more comfortably. Exoskeletons support people's bodies while they are working. The AI enhances that support by sensing a person's body and environment. It suggests ways to move better to reduce stress on the body. It also provides more power to help a person lift heavy objects.

AI is very helpful in manufacturing. But its usefulness is also limited. People still need to program AI and give it jobs to do. AI will continue to work side by side with people in the future.

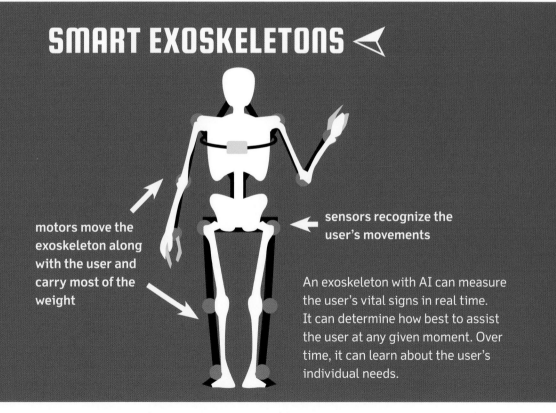

SMART EXOSKELETONS

motors move the exoskeleton along with the user and carry most of the weight

sensors recognize the user's movements

An exoskeleton with AI can measure the user's vital signs in real time. It can determine how best to assist the user at any given moment. Over time, it can learn about the user's individual needs.

CHAPTER 5

POLICE, FIRE, RESCUE, AND AI

Emergency services use AI in a variety of ways. For instance, robots with AI are slowly making their way into the police force. In India, for example, robot receptionists are helping people in police stations. They record people's complaints and direct them where they need to go. Other robots around the world analyze crime scene evidence. And small robots are doing **surveillance**. They record audio and video.

A robot with AI patrols the sidewalk in Beijing, China. It can recognize faces and detect fires.

Police departments can send them into places where criminals with guns are located. The robots send back information. They can listen in on conversations. They can record the layout of rooms. In some cases, the robots can even fight the criminals.

Some fire departments are using AI to fight wildfires. AI programs predict how wildfires will behave. By using satellite images and weather data, they predict the paths of fires. This information helps firefighters determine the starting point of the fire. It also helps them figure out where to send resources to help put out fires.

AI can perform jobs that are too dangerous for people. For example, militaries use robots with AI to defuse bombs. Robots are also becoming popular in rescue operations. They send information about disaster victims back to human

Militaries and police forces can use the TALON robot to dispose of bombs.

rescuers. They tell rescuers where people may be trapped. Robots with AI can even drop supplies to help victims until they can be rescued.

AI has a lot of potential to save and protect lives. But many people do not trust AI programs to make the best decisions in an emergency. AI programs cannot feel guilt or empathy toward people. Until people fully trust it, AI may only be a tool to help people in emergencies.

ROBIN MURPHY

Dr. Robin Murphy is a leader in AI rescue robotics. In 1992, she became the first person to receive a doctorate in robotics from the Georgia Institute of Technology. Dr. Murphy later became the director of the Center for Robot-Assisted Search and Rescue, or CRASAR. This organization studies disasters and the needs of rescuers.

Dr. Murphy's work involves identifying ways that AI can help in rescue operations. For example, AI programs can process large amounts of data quickly. They can deliver this data to rescuers to make their jobs easier. But one challenge is improving the communication among different AI programs working on the same emergency. Automated drones can figure out where people in danger may be located. But they must be able to fly in the same space as other rescue vehicles without crashing.

Robin Murphy talks to the press during a rescue mission.

Dr. Murphy has used her robots in many rescue efforts. Her robots helped sift through the rubble of the World Trade Center after the terrorist attacks on September 11, 2001. It was the first time rescue robots were ever used. Her robots also helped during Hurricane Wilma in 2004 and Hurricane Katrina in 2005. In addition, they safely checked the damage from the Fukushima Daiichi nuclear disaster in Japan in 2011.

CHAPTER 6

LIVING WITH AI

More and more, people are living among AI programs. AI helps people in their daily lives. Some AI programs resemble people. Other AI programs are in small devices. Still others exist inside the cars people drive. And some are inside the games that people play on their computers.

The most common robots inside people's homes are vacuum robots such as the Roomba. The Roomba looks like a disk. It has three buttons.

Some robots with AI look and act like pets.

Each one indicates the size of the room it should clean. Once a user pushes a button, the Roomba vacuums the floor all by itself. It senses its environment and avoids obstacles as it works.

Other robots with AI act as companions to people. They help with a variety of tasks. For instance, they check on members of the family. They remind the elderly to take their medications. If people ask the robots questions, the robots will find the answers. These robots can play music or control the temperature in the home. Some of them look like machines, while others look human.

Many people carry, use, or wear small devices with AI every day. The most popular is the smartphone. Virtual assistants on smartphones recognize voices and respond to questions and commands. Music apps such as Pandora play music and choose new music based on what a

▲ Some vacuum robots work on both carpet and hardwood. Some can even mop the floor.

person likes. The WT2 translator fits in the ear. The AI translates what it hears into a language the wearer understands.

AI exists inside the video games people play. AI software makes games seem very realistic.

◤ Virtual assistants such as Alexa can respond to people's commands and questions.

Non-player characters (NPCs) are characters generated by the computer that people can interact with in games. They are like robots with AI that live in the virtual world instead of the physical one. NPCs are designed to react like real people would when a player interacts with them.

Some cars are also equipped with AI. For example, a driverless car does not need a human driver. Instead, it has a computer brain. GPS, sensors, and cameras tell the computer about its location and environment. The computer then figures out what action to take if, for example, a traffic light turns red.

Other cars that are not driverless still use AI. For example, some cars can make sure the driver is healthy and not **intoxicated**. Cameras inside the car take images of the driver. The AI program looks at the images. It compares them to images of intoxicated drivers. It warns the driver if there is a match. The same cameras and AI make sure children, pets, and possessions are not left in a car by accident. AI can also check systems in a car to ensure the vehicle is working properly.

THINK ABOUT IT ◄

Cameras and AI are helping drivers stay safe. What might be one disadvantage of having cameras and AI inside your car?

CHAPTER 7

CREATIVE AI

Some AI programs are gaining the ability to be creative. For example, some AI programs can now compose their own music. They can take other people's music and sing and dance to it. Other AI programs can create works of art. AI software can be useful in film editing. And AI programs can write both news articles and works of fiction.

AI software has been used in film editing and movie-trailer production.

An AI called Aiva creates classical music. It studies music, learns common characteristics of music, and then composes new music based on what it has learned. Another AI called Hatsune Miku can perform any music she is given. This virtual character tours around the world. She is a **hologram** that sings and dances to songs for audiences. Human musicians accompany her.

AI programs can also create their own art. In 2018, an AI program painted a portrait of a fictional person named Edmond de Belamy. The painting sold for more than $400,000. A company called Obvious Art created the AI. The AI has two separate parts. The "Generator" first studied thousands of portraits from the 1300s to the 1900s. Then it made its own images. The "Discriminator" then compared the images to human-made works. The program was successful

▲ Hatsune Miku performs in front of a large crowd in Shanghai, China, in 2016.

when the Discriminator couldn't tell whether a human or the Generator had made the images.

Film editors are making use of AI as well. In particular, they are using it to help create movie trailers. In 2016, an AI program named Watson helped edit a trailer for a horror movie. Filmmakers first fed Watson the audio and video from many horror movies. Watson learned how to pick important scenes from these movies. It then found important scenes for the new trailer.

Normally, a trailer takes weeks to make. With Watson, it took only one day.

AI programs have also accomplished much in literature and journalism. In 2017, author Ross Goodwin took his AI software with him on a road trip across the United States. Along the way, he fed it hundreds of novels. He also gave it photos and the locations of places he traveled. By the end of the trip, the AI program had written a novel called *1 the Road*. In 2014, journalist Ken Schwencke created an AI program to report news about earthquakes. The AI Quakebot read data about earthquakes around the world. It then wrote

> ## ➤ THINK ABOUT IT
> Why do you think AI has to be fed many samples of art or music before it can create something new?

▲ The cofounder of Obvious Art stands by the AI-created portrait of Edmond de Belamy.

a real report that was published in the *Los Angeles Times*.

From creative projects to manufacturing plants, AI has made its mark on human life. As AI technology continues to advance, computers will help humans with even more tasks. AI can do some amazing things. However, it does have its limitations. In the future, AI and humans will work side by side, complementing each other to make the world a better place.

FOCUS ON
AI IN THE REAL WORLD

Write your answers on a separate piece of paper.

1. Write a letter to a friend describing the different ways people live with AI every day.

2. Which application of AI do you consider the most important? Why?

3. Which of the following is true about AI in health care?

    A. Robots with AI perform surgeries without human supervision.
    B. People can find new medications faster than AI programs can.
    C. Robots with AI carry supplies for doctors and nurses in hospitals.

4. Why might some workers oppose having AI in manufacturing plants?

    A. They might worry that they will lose their jobs to AI.
    B. They might worry that AI cannot work as quickly.
    C. They might worry about the robot's safety as it lifts heavy objects.

Answer key on page 48.

GLOSSARY

android
A robot with a human appearance.

automated
Operated by machines with minimal human input.

chatbots
Computer programs that talk to people.

exoskeletons
Devices strapped to and worn on the outside of the body.

hologram
A three-dimensional picture that is produced by lasers.

interactive
Able to respond to a user's actions or commands.

intoxicated
Under the influence of drugs or alcohol.

manufacturing
The making of goods by manual labor or machinery.

obstacles
Things that block someone's way.

pharmaceutical
Related to the making, using, or selling of medicinal drugs.

programmers
People who create, add, or change the instructions in a computer program.

surveillance
Close observation or monitoring.

TO LEARN MORE

BOOKS

Hulick, Kathryn. *Artificial Intelligence*. Minneapolis: Abdo Publishing, 2016.

McPherson, Stephanie Sammartino. *Artificial Intelligence: Building Smarter Machines*. Minneapolis: Twenty-First Century Books, 2018.

Negishi, Michiro. *My Cell Phone Can Think: A Textbook on Artificial Intelligence*. Milford, CT: Neuroverb, 2018.

NOTE TO EDUCATORS

Visit **www.focusreaders.com** to find lesson plans, activities, links, and other resources related to this title.

INDEX